BE ENCOURAGED

SPEAK THE WORD OF GOD

FOLAKE HASSAN

The Righteous Publishing House

London UK

BE ENCOURAGED

ISBN: 978-0-9928684-5-1

Published by The Righteous Publishing House

Flat 7, 93 Villiers Road

Willesden. London NW2 5QB

Visit Our Website at: www.theblessedchristian.co.uk

APPRECIATION

I give all praises to God Almighty, who chose me and qualified me to be a Christian. I thank God for empowered me to study His Word and for blessing me with His Wisdom. My sincere appreciation also goes to the men and women from every part of the world that God has used to minister His Words to bless me. I thank my children for their good attitude that have enabled me to walk a good walk in my journey as a Christian. I thank my parents for taking good care of me through my childhood and they still do today.

Table of Contents

Introduction

This book has been written to encourage someone not to give up on their God's given assignment, it is to encourage someone to rise and be the best God has purposed them to be. We thank God for His Words, the counsel of God is more than enough for each and every one of us in the Name of Jesus Christ. We can all get good encouragements from the Word of God, we must allow the Word of God to dwell in us richly.

We must not allow anything to make us feel as if we are less than what God created us to be, your colour is not a barrier, your gender is not a barrier, your accent is not a barrier, your educational qualifications is not a barrier, your financial status is not a barrier and your marital status is not a barrier.

The resources God deposited in you is sufficient for you to start your God's given assignments. You are not inferior to anyone, you may not have the same charisma as other people in your profession, that does not mean that you are not unique on your own. Be willing to develop the Gift of God within you.

1

Learn from this book, the good practical steps you can take to gain good confidence in Christ.

Chapter 1

SPEAK THE WORD OF GOD

And they said to all the company of
Israelites, The land through which we
passed as scouts is an exceedingly good
land. If the Lord delights in us, then He
will bring us into this land and give it to
us, a land flowing with milk and honey
(Numbers 14:7-8)

For anyone to receive the blessing of the Lord, they must desired it, they must crave for it, so was the story of the two men who went with eight others to go and spied out The Promised Land God promised the Children of Israel. Satan and the wrong systems, wrong imaginations and every wrong doctrines will try to have access into anyone's lives as long as they permit it within their thinking, but it shouldn't be so. It is about the time when The Children of God should decide to study The Bible to find out the Truth about God and what He is saying about their situations.

3

*Tell them, as I live, says the Lord, what
you have said in My hearing I will do to
you (Numbers 14:28)*

The Word of God carries within it so much revelations, relevance's and blessings, hence the reasons why some ungodly nations tries to hide it from their citizens so as to keep them ignorant and keep them in the states of begging for their rights, but it must not be so.

Moses as The leader God chose, to lead the Israelites out of Egypt, appointed leaders to go and searched the Promised Land God promised to give to the Israelites. On their returns from the journey, some of the leaders gave a bad report of the land which they went to searched due to ignorance, whilst two men among them by the name Caleb and Joshua gave a good report that they are capable of entering the Promised Land to possess it as God promised them (see Numbers 13:30). May I encourage someone to learn to have absolute trust in God always concerning all His good promises whether it be for your healing or for your prosperities? God is not a man, He will not tell a lie, and all His promises to us should be yes and amen to all believers. Our focused should always be on Gods promises as it is in The Bible, and not on what someone says, especially if it is contrary to The Truth of The Word of God. God advices that He doesn't want anyone slothful in His business, but those fervent in spirit serving The Lord, it means that we must all be diligent in our studying the Word of God, we must give ourselves to studying the Word. Christian Faith is not for the lazy people, it is not for those that will not do anything but waiting for someone to spoon-feed them all their lives, someone may spoon-feed you whilst you are a baby Christian, but a time should come when you will choose to set time apart to study The Word of God for yourself. We must all choose to study the Word of God to find out His promises for us as His chosen ones, it must become our lifestyle habit to study The Word of God.

The Word of God will empower us to say good things about ourselves, it will empower us to say good things about our spouse, it will empower us to say good things about our children, it will empower us to say good things about our family and friends, and it will empower us to confess the faithfulness of God. The Bible advices us to allow the Word of God to dwell in us richly, so that our lips can confess its faithfulness. There is power in our words, the Bible says a man's belly will be satisfied with the fruit of his lips (Proverbs 18:20), it means that you will conceived, become and received what you constantly says, get the Word of God and allow it to fill your spirit, Soul and body, and what you will manifest will be God's goodness all the days of your life, and the Word of God shall become your defence in the day of trouble. If God is leading you, you need not fear any human being or their systems, the Word of God carries within it enough power to manifest God's goodness, the Word of God can make the beasts that supposed to destroy you to be in league with you, it can empowers the king, the queen and the government to works in your favour.

"Blessed is the one whom God corrects; so do not despise the discipline of the Almighty. For He wounds, but He also binds up; He injures, but His hands also heal.
From six calamities He will rescue you; in seven no harm will touch you. In famine He will deliver you from death, and in battle from the stroke of the sword.
You will be protected from the lash of the tongue, and need not fear when destruction comes. You will laugh at destruction and famine, and need not fear

the wild animals.
For you will have a covenant with the stones of the field, and the wild animals will be at peace with you. You will know that your tent is secure; you will take stock of your property and find nothing missing.
You will know that your children will be many, and your descendants like the grass of the earth. You will come to the grave in full vigour, like sheaves gathered in season. "We have examined this, and it is true.
So hear it and apply it to yourself."
(Job 5:17-27) NIV

Happy and *fortunate is the man whom God reproves; so do not despise or reject the correction of the Almighty [subjecting you to trial and suffering]. For He wounds, but He binds up; He smites, but His hands heal. He will rescue you in six troubles; in seven nothing that is evil [for you] will touch you. In famine He will redeem you from death, and in war from the power of the sword. You shall be hidden from the scourge of the tongue, neither shall you be afraid of destruction when it comes. At destruction and famine you shall laugh, neither shall you be afraid of the living creatures of the earth. For you shall be in*

7

*league with the stones of the field, and
the beasts of the field shall be at peace
with you. And you shall know that your
tent shall be in peace, and you shall visit
your fold and your dwelling and miss
nothing [from them]. You shall know also
that your children shall be many, and your
offspring as the grass of the earth. You
shall come to your grave in ripe old age,
and as a shock of grain goes up [to the
threshing floor] in its season. This is what
we have searched out; it is true.
Hear and heed it and know for yourself
[for your good] (Job 5: 17-27) AMP.*

The system may have trained you on how to confess evils, it may have trained you how to confess negative or it may have filled you with all kind of fears, but you do not need to die as a slave with any ungodly system, choose life, and choose the Word of God.

It pleases God whenever we say what He says and it displeases God whenever we did not say what He says. Allow the Word of God to dwell in you richly, to flow to you through your eyes and through your hears (Matthew 6:22 & Exodus 15:26), allow the Word of God to fill your beings, allow it to flow through your thinking faculties. The Bible advices that as a man thinks in his heart so is he, this planet is not for the lazy people, therefore we must all set times apart to make sure we are all loaded with the Word of God daily, we must allow the Word of God to guide us into all truth. God Himself sets the examples in the first two chapters of the Bible by creating the world with His spoken Words, and the Bible advices that The Word of God is God Himself and without Him was nothing made.

In the beginning [before all time] was the Word (Christ), and the Word was with God, and the Word was God Himself. He was present originally with God. All things were made and came into existence through Him; and without Him was not even one thing made that has come into being. In Him was Life, and the Life was the Light of men. And the Light shines on in the darkness, for the darkness has never overpowered it [put it out or absorbed it or appropriated it, and is unreceptive to it] (John 1:1-5)

He who believes in Me [who cleaves to and trusts in and relies on Me] as the Scripture has said, from his innermost being shall flow [continuously] springs and rivers of living water (John 7:38)

What God requires from each and every one of us is for us to allow the Word of God to dwell in us richly and flow through us easily, He wants it to become normal things to say and do what God says.

Jesus Christ set us some good examples by emphasising that He only do and say what He saw His Father doing and what His Father taught Him, and as Christians, thank God for the Father God, for we do not hold our birth right to the blood and flesh only but to The Spirit of The Living God, for it is in God we have our beings, in Him we move and in Him we live. Therefore the Word of God must not depart from our lips, we must all be born again by The Spirit of The Living God that dwells within us.

> But to as many as did receive and welcome Him, He gave the authority (power, privilege, right) to become the children of God, that is, to those who believe in (adhere to, trust in, and rely on) His name— Who owe their birth neither to bloods nor to the will of the flesh [that of physical impulse] nor to the will of man [that of a natural father], but to God. [They are born of God!] And the Word (Christ) became flesh (human, incarnate) and tabernacled (fixed His tent of flesh, lived awhile) among us; and we [actually]

saw His glory (His honour, His majesty),
such glory as an only begotten son receives
from his father, full of grace (favour,
loving-kindness) and truth.   (John 1:12-
14)

John 1: 12-14 is not intended to make children not to honour their biological parents, in fact the Bible makes honouring our parents one of the topmost in God's commandments to us, but what we are to learn from these particular verses is that God's Word must be the number one priority in our lives because it is capable of preparing us to honour our parents. If you honour God, you will be able to honour your parents.

Honour your father and your mother, as
the Lord your God commanded you, that
your days may be prolonged and that it
may go well with you in the land which
the Lord your God gives you (Deuteronomy
5:16)

We are first of all the Spirit being before we manifest in the flesh, we were originally with God before we manifest in the flesh (see John 1:2) We owe our birth right to God first before our biological parents, therefore both parents and their children must be born again of The Spirit of The Living God from

11

where we all originates. Therefore God is our Father, therefore God is the one who gave us to our biological parents. It is the Word of God we must first and foremost chase and allow to dwell in us richly to illuminate and guide us into all truth, it is capable of making us to be well and fit enough to take good care of ourselves and our family including our biological parents, a child that is doing well is the joy of his/her parents. Whoever has the Word of God has everything in this life and in the life to come.

> *In fact, I greatly rejoiced when [some of] the brethren from time to time arrived and spoke [so highly] of the sincerity and fidelity of your life, as indeed you do live in the Truth [the whole Gospel presents].* **I have no greater joy than this, to hear that my [spiritual] children are living their lives in the Truth** *(3 John 1:3-4)*

> *It is the Spirit Who gives life [He is the Life-giver]; the flesh conveys no benefit whatever [there is no profit in it]. The words (truths) that I have been speaking to you are spirit and life (John 6:63)*

Therefore, we must seek the Kingdom of God first, and every other things shall be added unto us.

Avoid anything and anyone that will not allow you to become the best God has destined you to be. Pray about all things and ask God to direct you in all your ways. Learn from Jesus Christ, He only speaks what God wanted Him to speak.

So Jesus answered them by saying, *I assure you, most solemnly I tell you, the Son is able to do nothing of Himself (of His own accord); but He is able to do only what He sees the Father doing, for whatever the Father does is what the Son does in the same way [in His turn] (John 5:19)*

So Jesus added, *When you have lifted up the Son of Man [on the cross], you will realize (know, understand) that I am He [for Whom you look] and that I do nothing of Myself (of My own accord or on My own authority), but I say [exactly] what My Father has taught Me. And He Who sent Me is ever with Me; My Father has not left Me alone, for I always do what pleases Him. (John 8:28-29)*

Do not be afraid to make mistakes in your pursuits of righteousness, settle it in your mind that if you make a mistake, the Lord God will perfect that which concerns you, He will give you the opportunity to get things right. Therefore the fear of making mistake should not paralyse anyone from becoming the best God destined them to become, be willing to learn, the more knowledge you have in your chosen field, the

13

more confidence you will become. Do not allow any fear or the tongues of men to cripple you.

Later on there was a Jewish festival (feast) for which Jesus went up to Jerusalem. Now there is in Jerusalem a pool near the Sheep Gate. This pool in the Hebrew is called Bethesda, having five porches (alcoves, colonnades, doorways). In these lay a great number of sick folk— some blind, some crippled, and some paralyzed (shrivelled up)—waiting for the bubbling up of the water. For an angel of the Lord went down at appointed seasons into the pool and moved and stirred up the water; whoever then first, after the stirring up of the water, stepped in was cured of whatever disease with which he was afflicted. There was a certain man there who had suffered with a deep-seated and lingering disorder for thirty-eight years. When Jesus noticed him lying there [helpless], knowing that he had already been a long time in that condition, He said to him, do you want to become well? [Are you really in earnest about getting well?] The invalid answered, Sir, I have nobody when the water is moving to put me into the pool; but while I am trying to come [into it] myself, somebody else steps down ahead of me.

Jesus said to him, Get up! Pick up your
bed (sleeping pad) and walk! (John 5: 1-8)

I don't really know how long you have tolerated people's opinions, ideas and your own personal imaginations to cripple you? Peoples opinion and personal imagination is when you think that you have to be like someone before you can be good enough for God's blessings, it is as if we are telling God, what has He made; as if we are telling God He has not created a wonderful being, and the Bible advices us not to do so, not to be like the Children of Israel that complained and did not honour God for all His goodness towards them on their journey from Egypt, but to learn and chooses to thank God while He is perfecting that which concerns us. Jesus is saying to someone today you have had enough of rejection and condemnation from every ungodly systems "Arise and Walk"

The Word of God is saying to someone today "you have dwelt long enough on this mountain. Arise, go and received your blessings in The Name of Jesus Christ by starting to allow the Word of God to dwell in you richly.

The Lord our God said to us in Horeb, You
have dwelt long enough on this mountain.
Turn and take up your journey and go to

*the hill country of the Amorites, and to all
their neighbours in the Arabah, in the hill
country, in the lowland, in the South (the
Negeb), and on the coast, the land of the
Canaanites, and Lebanon, as far as the
great river, the river Euphrates. Behold, I
have set the land before you; go in and
take possession of the land which the Lord
swore to your fathers, to Abraham, to
Isaac, and to Jacob, to give to them and to
their descendants after them
(Deuteronomy 1: 6-8)*

Scriptures to encourage us that God has Not Given unto Us the Spirit of Fear but to declare The Word of God:

*Till I come, devote yourself to [public and
private] reading, to exhortation
(preaching and personal appeals), and to
teaching and instilling doctrine (1 Timothy
4:13)*

*For God did not give us a spirit of timidity
(of cowardice, of craven and cringing and
fawning fear), but [He has given us a
spirit] of power and of love and of
calm and well-balanced*

mind and discipline and self-control (2
Timothy 1:7)

He that is fearful has not been made perfect in love, for perfect love cast fears out of the door.

There is no fear in love [dread does not exist], but full-grown (complete, perfect) love turns fear out of doors and expels every trace of terror! For fear brings with it the thought of punishment, and [so] he who is afraid has not reached the full maturity of love [is not yet grown into love's complete perfection] (1 John 4: 18)

God Himself speak the world into existence by His spoken word.

Now faith is the assurance (the confirmation, the title deed) of the things [we] hope for, being the proof of things [we] do not see and the conviction of their reality [faith perceiving as real fact what is not revealed to the senses]. For by [faith—trust and holy fervour born of faith] the men of old had divine testimony borne to them and obtained a good report. By faith we understand that the worlds [during the successive ages] were framed (fashioned, put in order, and equipped for their intended purpose) by

the word of God, so that what we see was
not made out of things which are visible
(Hebrews 11:1-3)

Why the Word of God?

***Everything that was created was created by the spoken Word of God.

***The Word of God gives confidence, when you are well versed with the word of God, no devil will be able to intimidate you.

***The Word of God gives competency, the Bible advices that a man that is competent in his profession will not stand before ordinary mean men but he will stand before the kings. It is good to have the sound knowledge of The Wisdom of God.

***If you have a good understanding of the Word of God, you will not find it difficult to obey God.

***No evil has ever overpowered the Word of God, the Word of God is the only Word that satan fears (John 1:1-5)

***God wants us to say what He says, He doesn't want us to become a liar, and a liar is anyone who says and confess what God has not says.

***A day will come when we may all have to take actions based on what we believe, God expects His chosen's one to know the right things to do and to take wise actions based on His Words (see Numbers 20:7-12)

***If you are well versed with the Word of God, if the Word of God dwells in you richly, you will obey God, it will become normal for you to do the right thing according to The Word of God.

Chapter 2

REJOICE IN THE LORD ALWAYS

Rejoice in the Lord always [delight,
gladden yourselves in Him]; again I say,
Rejoice! (Philippians 4:4)

Rejoicing in the Lord is when you allowed the Word of God to dwell in you richly to flush away from you anything that is not healthy, to flush away from you wrong opinion of men of you, to flush away from you every spirit of fear. Rejoicing in The Lord is when you allowed the Word of God to give you the confidence that is necessary for all your endeavours. Rejoicing in The Lord is acknowledging the Lordship of Jesus Christ over situations. Rejoicing in the Lord does not necessarily means jumping up and down in dancing, but knowing and having the Truth of the Word of God dwelling in you richly to the extent that no weapons formed by satan will have power over you, it is having the Word of God in you abundantly to settle all matters.

The Word of God emphasises that we are all beautiful for our situations that we are fearfully and wonderfully made in The Image of God. On a daily basis we should declare to ourselves "I shall not die as a mediocre in The Name of Jesus Christ but manifesting the best God has created me to be"

Rejoicing in the Lord is when you have allowed the faithfulness of God to heal you, to make you to be wealthy, healthy and prosperous until it overflows to those around you.

Celebrate God all day, every day. I mean, revel in him! Make it as clear as you can to all you meet that you're on their side, working with them and not against them........
(Philippians 4:4) **The Message.**

Stop Comparing Yourself to Others

The Bible says that any time the Christians compare themselves with one another, they are not wise, and I don't think it is a good thing for anyone to fall into the categories of the foolish in the kingdom of God. God has made each and every one of us unique to fit into His good purpose for each and every one of us. We must slow down to thank God for what He has made us to be for Him, trusting that at the appropriate time He will perfect that which concerns us, and not running up and down all our lives wanting to be like someone else, when are we going to slow down to enjoy and start appreciating what God has already provided for us. It is not a crime to always study the best examples in our society and desire to be better than them, God may not make you to be able to deliver a particular task the way someone is delivering it in your community. God may not change the colour of your skin, that may not be what God will do for you, while you are on your way to perfection, do not allow anything to cast you down and cast you out of this planet by telling you how not too good for them you are, you may not be perfect for everyone on this planet, but God has never created a junk, therefore I say unto you "you are beautiful" and for men I say "you are handsome". Do not despise the day of your small beginnings. Your ascent is beautiful, your colour is beautiful and your height is wonderful. I love the response David gave to king Saul, when king Saul was trying to belittle the grace of God on David:

> *And Saul said to David, You are not able to go to fight against this Philistine. You are only an adolescent, and he has been a*

warrior from his youth. And David said to Saul, Your servant kept his father's sheep. And when there came a lion or again a bear and took a lamb out of the flock. I went out after it and smote it and delivered the lamb out of its mouth; and when it arose against me, I caught it by its beard and smote it and killed it. Your servant killed both the lion and the bear; and this uncircumcised Philistine shall be like one of them, for he has defied the armies of the living God! David said, The Lord Who delivered me out of the paw of the lion and out of the paw of the bear, He will deliver me out of the hand of this Philistine. And Saul said to David, Go, and the Lord be with you! (1 Samuel 17:33-37)

That is what I call A God's kind of Spirit, the spirit that will not give up, the spirit that will not allow anyone or anything to make them think that they are inferior or that they cannot attain the greater height God purposed for them. The Spirit that will confront every wrong teachings in our midst, the Spirit that will terminate every wrong spirit in our mind.

If it were the children of today, only God knows what would have been their response to king Saul, they could look for a corner to sob and accept their defeat straightaway, but David refused to accept the kings

24

conclusion of him that he cannot conquered the goliath..

God may not make you to be like the people you compared yourself with, their gifting's may not be the best God has for you. The Children of Israel though being in the Egypt thought their condition was normal, some of them thought they had the best, which showed in their attitudes towards God in the wilderness by complaining and regretting leaving Egypt (Numbers 14:1-3), but a day came when God visited their situations and brought them out of Egypt, on their way to the Promised Land some of them complained that they missed their lifestyle in Egypt. Some said they wish they could be in Egypt, because there they get their foods and other basic amenities, but to God life is more them the food and the basic amenities.

Instead of comparing yourself to other people at all times, study the Word of God and other Christian Books God will placed in your hands, allow the Word of God to illuminate and direct you into your own unique blessings in The Name of Jesus Christ.

Just like David, we must choose to remind ourselves regularly of how God has been faithful to us, we must not allow any voices, any faces or any imaginations to keep reminding us of our inabilities to become the best for God's blessings. We must remembered how David took his stands and says, I have come here to win and not to lose. Anything, including the government, the systems, financial situations, and imaginations may try to buy you out of your miracles, you are the one who will make up your mind and choose to fight the good fight of faith until you are truly manifesting the blessings of The Lord everywhere you go, until the whole world will have nothing wrong to say about you, until they start paying you to seek the Wisdom of God in you because of the Godly attitudes you manifest everywhere you go.

SAY THIS OUT LOUD

I am beautiful for my situations

I am not inferior, I have God's superior Spirit in me

My identity is in Christ Jesus and not in people's opinions of me

I am fearfully and wonderfully made

I am not a failure, I am a success

God has not given me the spirit of fear, but that of power, love and of a sound mind

I can do all things through Christ Who strengthens me

My colour is not a barrier

My gender is not a barrier

My height is not a barrier

My ascent is not a barrier

My educational qualifications in not a barrier

I have what I need to manifest the blessings of The Lord in life.

My labour shall not be a waste, I shall be a partaker of my good initiatives in The Name of Jesus Christ.

INSTANCES FROM THE BIBLE

The Story of Moses

The Children of Israel found themselves in the land of Egypt for a several years. God promised to bring them out into His Promised Blessings for them, and

God purposed to carry out the assignment through a man called Moses.

Right from inception, satan sowed the wrong seed of fear and inabilities in the mind of Moses to the extent that Moses felt he was not good enough for the assignment (Exodus 4:10), God in spite of Moses negative behaviour chose to used Moses. The journey began and the Children of Israel were lead out of Egypt by Moses, it got to a point where God wanted Moses to speak to the challenges confronting them, instead of Moses speaking the Word of God, he chose to do something different to the instructions given to him by the Lord and Moses action displeases God. I pray that no one among us will offend God by allowing fear and wrong thinking's to dominate us, no weapons formed by satan will have authority over us in Jesus Name.

The Story of Esther

Esther was a woman who chose to obey God in the face of danger, she was an orphan and a foreigner (a Jew) in the country called Persia, because God was on her side, she won the contest and she became the queen and got married to king Ahasuerus. Despite all the efforts involved to win as a queen, her battle did not finished there, she had to take the bold steps to stop all The Jews in the region from being wiped out by death, she applied the Wisdom of God to the situation and the death sentence over all the Jews was nullified by God.

Esther could have complained about the fact that she was an orphan, maybe just about to be getting healed from the pain of losing her parents, she could have complained about the fact that being a foreigner, the king may discriminate against her, but she did not allowed anything to stop her life from being blessed, she encouraged herself plus the encouragements she received from her uncle and put herself forward as a queen, and she won the contest.

Therefore, there should not be any force or tongue that is big enough to stop your life from being blessed.

For more instances from the Bible, see the stories of Joseph and David.

God is sending you on assignment, never refused Him, and never says you are not competent enough if it is God sending you. Never complain about your colour, race, gender, height, accents, or lack of educational qualification. What looks like your inabilities may be the abilities God has placed in you to make you unique, it may be the only thing that will distinguish you for blessings. Pray to God to give you the boldness to deliver His message, pray to God and ask for the good gifts of utterance.

> And [pray] also for me, that [freedom of]
> utterance may be given me, that I may
> open my mouth to proclaim boldly the
> mystery of the good news (the Gospel).
> .... Pray] that I may declare it
> boldly and courageously, as I ought to do
> (Ephesians 6: 19-20)

SAVE YOUR LIFE AND LIVES OF OTHERS BY CHOOSING TO BELIEVE GOD AND TO SPEAK HIS WORDS

Trust God that if He is the one who began a good work in you, He will perfect it.

The Bible advices us not to be afraid of people's faces. As for our mouth, God promises to be with our mouth, He promised that we shall open our mouth and He will speak through us.

> But the Lord said to me, Say not, I am only
> a youth; for you shall go to all to whom I

shall send you, and whatever I command
you, you shall speak. Be not afraid of
them [their faces], for I am with you to
deliver you, says the Lord. Then the Lord
put forth His hand and touched my mouth.
And the Lord said to me, Behold, I have
put My words in your mouth (Jeremiah
1:7-9)

LEARN FROM GOD

God spoke the earth into existence through His Spoken Word and the Bible says The Word we speak they are Spirit and life and that The Word of God is God Himself (John 1:1)

Speaking The Word of God is Very Important.

The Bible says: whosoever shall say unto this mountain, be removed.................. It is better to allow people to mock you than not to do the will of God.

People may comments about your personalities, but never allow that to make you to surrender your destiny into the hands of your enemies.

Beware who you give your ears.

****Be prepared for people to make all kinds of comments about your good action for God.

****Remembered, Jesus response to them, "Father, forgive them for they know not what they do" (Luke 23:34)

**God will turn around to favour you what seems like your inabilities, by you accepting the abilities of God, Nations shall celebrate you.

**The Lord God will turn your source of ridicules to become your source of miracle.

**The fact that it seems that you are not capable should be the reason why you should keep trying to be the best God created you to be until you are perfect.

SPEAK THE WORD OF GOD

Find time to study the Word of God and other subjects that relates to your destiny, be well versed with the Word of God.

Scriptures To Encourage Us To Be Strong in The Lord

The Jews were astonished. They said, How is it that this Man has learning [is so versed in the sacred Scriptures and in theology] when He has never studied? (John 7:15)

The upright (honourable, intrinsically good) man out of the good treasure [stored] in his heart produces what is upright (honourable and intrinsically good), and the evil man out of the evil storehouse brings forth that which is depraved (wicked and intrinsically evil); for out of the abundance (overflow) of the heart his mouth speaks. (Luke 6:45)

Therefore, [there is] now no condemnation (no adjudging guilty of wrong) for those who are in Christ Jesus, who live [and] walk not after the dictates of the flesh, but after the dictates of the Spirit. For the law of the Spirit of life [which is] in Christ Jesus [the law of our new being] has freed me from the law of sin and of death (Romans 8:1-2)

*I have strength for all things in Christ Who
empowers me [I am ready for anything and
equal to anything through Him
Who infuses inner strength into me; I
am self-sufficient in Christ's sufficiency]
Phil.4:13) Amp.*

*I can do all things through Christ which
strengthened me (Phil.4:13) KJV*

****FOCUSED ON GOD AND ON YOUR ASSIGNMENTS

****CONFESING THE WORD OF GOD ALL THROUGH

****SAY WHAT GOD SAYS NOT WHAT THE DEVIL SAYS

Allow the Word of God to dwell in you richly, then you will defeat all the wrong voices and every wrong imaginations that comes against you.

PERSISTENT AND FOCUSING ON THE WORD OF GOD IS THE KEY TO CONQUER FEARS AND EVERY FORM OF INABILITIES

The Word of God must not depart from you, you must meditate on it, you must listen to it, and you must ponder over it.

INSTANCES IN THE BIBLE WHERE GOD OVERULES THE SPIRIT OF SATANIC DISCOURAGEMENTS

Instead of telling God, you cannot do it, learn from King David in The Bible in his preparation to meet Goliath, everything tried to distract and discouraged him, but David gave some good answers, check his response to king Saul and his brothers (1 Samuel 17:23-37)

The woman at the well tries to discourage Jesus Christ Himself, but Jesus answered her: If you had only known and had recognized God's gift and Who this is that is saying to you, Give Me a drink, you would have asked Him [instead] and He would have given you living water (John 4:10)

And when he was come into his own country, he taught them in their synagogue, insomuch that they were astonished, and said, whence hath this

35

*man this wisdom, and these mighty works?
Is not this the carpenter's son? Is not his
mother called Mary? And his brethren,
James, and Joses, and Simon, and Judas?
And his sisters, are they not all with us?
Whence then hath this man all these
things? (Matthew 13: 54-56)*

*Therefore there arose a controversy
between some of John's disciples and a
Jew in regard to purification. So they
came to John and reported to him, Rabbi,
the Man Who was with you on the other
side of the Jordan [at the Jordan
crossing]—and to Whom you yourself have
borne testimony—notice, here He is
baptizing too, and everybody is flocking to
Him! John answered, A man can receive
nothing [he can claim nothing, he can take
unto himself nothing] except as it has
been granted to him from heaven. [A man
must be content to receive the gift which
is given him from heaven; there is no
other source.] (John 3:25-27)*

*I am the true vine, and my Father is the
husbandman. Every branch in me that
beareth not fruit he taketh away: and
every branch that beareth fruit, he
purgeth it, that it may bring forth more
fruit. Now ye are clean through the word*

*which I have spoken unto you. Abide in
me, and I in you. As the branch cannot
bear fruit of itself, except it abide in the
vine; no more can ye, except ye abide in
me. I am the vine, ye are the branches: He
that abideth in me, and I in him, the same
bringeth forth much fruit: for without me
ye can do nothing. If a man abide not in
me, he is cast forth as a branch, and is
withered; and men gather them, and cast
them into the fire, and they are burned. If
ye abide in me, and my words abide in
you, ye shall ask what ye will, and it shall
be done unto you. (John 15: 1-7) KJV*

*I am the True Vine, and My Father is the
Vinedresser. Any branch in Me that does
not bear fruit [that stops bearing] He cuts
away (trims off, takes away); and He
cleanses and repeatedly prunes every
branch that continues to bear fruit, to
make it bear more and richer and more
excellent fruit. You are
cleansed and pruned already, because of
the word which I have given you [the
teachings I have discussed with you].
Dwell in Me, and I will dwell in you. [Live
in Me, and I will live in you.] Just as no
branch can bear fruit of itself without
abiding in (being vitally united to) the
vine, neither can you bear fruit unless you*

37

abide in Me. I am the Vine; you are the branches. Whoever lives in Me and I in him bears much (abundant) fruit. However, apart from Me [cut off from vital union with Me] you can do nothing. If a person does not dwell in Me, he is thrown out like a [broken-off] branch, and withers; such branches are gathered up and thrown into the fire, and they are burned. If you live in Me [abide vitally united to Me] and My words remain in you and continue to live in your hearts, ask whatever you will, and it shall be done for you. When you bear (produce) much fruit, My Father is honoured and glorified, and you show and prove yourselves to be true followers of Mine. (John 15: 1-8)

Chapter 3

BE HEALED IN THE NAME OF JESUS CHRIST

*...... for there is no distinction between
Jew and Greek. The same Lord is Lord
over all [of us] and He generously bestows
His riches upon all who call upon Him [in
faith] (Romans 10:12)*

Receive your healing in the Name of Jesus Christ
from every form of sickness and abuse, pick up your
bed and start walking. Do not allow the past to cripple
your future anymore, do not give satan the authority
to rule over you. Be willing to become the best God
destined you to be, just like the Children of Israel, be
willing to relocate to another geographical location if
God is directing you to do so.

You Will Always Need Jesus

There are roles you will play and there are some roles God has to play, you must settle it in your mind that after you have played your own role, to trust God for the blessings.

Jesus answered him, Go in peace; your son will live! And the man put his trust in what Jesus said and started home......... Then the father knew that it was at that very hour when Jesus had said to him, your son will live. And he and his entire household believed (adhered to, trusted in, and relied on Jesus). (John 4:50 & 53)

It Is Not Too Late

Is anything too hard or too wonderful for the Lord........ (Genesis 18:14)

God's response to Sarah when she wondered at the promises of God for her to conceive and delivered a child after being old was "is there anything too hard for God" and at the appropriate time God came through for her, she conceived and gave birth to a child.

No one can be too old to be blessed by the Lord, no one can be too old to start studying the Word of God. We heard the testimony of a retired cleaner with no academic qualifications, who started and own a school.

Abraham and Sarah passed the age of child bearing, God still chose to give them Children.

If you cannot start your own venture, chose to join those that are doing something good and God will still blesses you and you will fulfilled destiny. David left behind the sheep, he went where God lead him, there he fought the Goliath and won the battle, also God led David to an anointing to become a king, every forces from the pit of hell kicked against David, especially the forces from his brothers, but God has purposed to make David to become king and David ignored every wrong voices and comments that came against him, he stood his ground to become who God ordained him to be.

I HOPE SOMEONE IS ENCOURAGED TO PERSEVERE, TO RISE UP AND DO SOMETHING GOOD. A million voices may be telling you how you are not capable, voices and wrong imaginations may tell you "we already have too many people in that particular vocation", but let the Word of God encourage you. I can assure you, God will send your way your own customers. If God gives the idea, there is a customer waiting for it.

A story that fascinate me was and is the story of Peter J Daniel, a man that was tagged as illiterate, a bricklayer, but he refused to give in to what the system wanted to retired him to, he chose to study and become one of the best life coach, my question is "What is your excuse"?

And David inquired of the Lord, saying, Shall I pursue this troop? Shall I overtake them? The Lord answered him, Pursue, for you shall surely overtake them and without fail recover all (1 Samuel 30:8)

I watched a video recently, where Peter J Daniel was still going about delivering his own summits at the age of eighty two years with several souls thanking him for his great contributions to their lives, so, what is someone's excuses?

Weeping is not the answer, and if you have any reason to weep for any loses of any kind, after the weeping has been done, start doing something good and constructive with your life. If you have enquired of the Lord about your plan, if God says to you to go forward, then be bold enough to go forward in your good plans. If a voice says to you "too many people are in that business" then you can say "maybe the service is in demand or it must be a good gesture and idea for many people to have been doing it" then go for it. If the voice says to you "no one is doing it, maybe it is not a good idea", you can reply by saying if not many people are doing it, then it may means there is a shortage of suppliers, go forward in your God's given ideas. I don't think there is any business or venture you are planning to launch that no one is doing already, what you can do to encourage yourself is to go forward and manifest the blessings the Lord has deposited in you.

I once listened to the videos of Peter J Daniel, in his early years in the ministry, several preparation usually took place for him to be able to deliver a sermon, but as he continued, God empowers him to conquered the fear of speaking in the public.

The Word of God is a good source of encouragements, study it by reading and by listening to it, it will empowers you not to faint in your preparation seasons. Be persevere in whatever God has called you to manifest for Him, have it at the back of your mind that your efforts shall be fruitful, your labour shall not be a waste in The Name of Jesus Christ.

In the story of David and the Israelites in 1 Samuel 30, David could have retired and accepted defeats and joined the mourners, but instead, David encouraged himself in the Lord, he pursued and recovered what was lost, so we must all have a good attitude to always be determined to win, to recover back what satan has stolen from this generation.

Do not look for helps all the times, choose to work to cultivate your own grounds, imagine what the praise report will be if a continent has to rely on another continents for all their needs or if they have to abandon their continents thinking of migrating to the prepared ground somewhere, it will means that we wouldn't have had some continents, but we thank God for all the continents and the men and women that chose to stay in their land to cultivate it, hence we have places where we can go on holidays and for businesses.

May I encourage someone to be willing to be diligent in their God's given assignments, to focus on their goals and to aspire to be successful. No talents is too small in the sight of God, be busy doing good, and at the appropriate time, God will give you a good reward, being busy in your God's give assignments will not kill you, it will only make you wiser and stronger.

*Do you see a man diligent and skilful in his
business? He will stand before kings; he
will not stand before obscure men
(Proverbs 22:29)*

People may laugh at you initially, you may not get it right initially, and you may not be able to say it the way someone else will say it, but as you continue using the faith God has given you, things will get better and better.

Chapter 4

START WITH WHAT YOU HAVE

........Your handmaid has nothing in the house except a jar of oil (2 Kings 4:3c)

For that business, for your God ordained ideas and purposes, you do not need to wait for another thirty eight years for your miracles to happen. Start with what you have, what you have may look insignificant to you, but with the help of the Holy Spirit, it is significant.

Remember the first thing Elisha said to the widow woman in 2 Kings 4 "what do you have in your house?" and her reply was "nothing.... but a jar of oil". Maybe what you have looks like nothing, but you do have something good and tangible, you have the ability to study the word of God, you have the ability to understand what you study to receive illuminations and encouragements, you have the ability to encourage someone, you have the ability to accept a meaningful employments.

If what you have is nothing, that is the reason why you should start doing something meaningful, your starting may lead you into having something, whatever your excuses, take it to the Lord in prayer.

PRAYER

May I asked you to pray for God's fresh oil to rest on you and give you the ability to become a good encourager to others too in The Name of Jesus Christ. I pray that the gifting of God in you shall not die and it will not waste in The Name of Jesus Christ. You will look around you and see that you are truly endowed with blessings. May the Lord empowered you to see His gifting's in you and for you to start using them. You will not need to wait for a further thirty years before you start doing something tangible and meaningful with the talent God has given you (see John 5:1-8). Your songs shall no longer be "I have no one to help me" but you will say "I can do all things through Christ Who strengthens me". The Lord God will remove from your life every satanic embargoes to your blessings, you will rise and shine for God, no evil will be able to put a wrong tag on you in The Name of Jesus Christ, sickness and death shall not be your portion.

The woman in 2 Kings 4 remembered that she has something (a jar of oil), because what the man of God is asking for is something that is of sale values according to the Bible, something that can generate income for her, something that can solve her financial needs and meet her needs. I pray that God will open someone's eyes and encourage them to start using what they have in The Name of Jesus Christ, to see the blessings of The Lord that surrounds them. May The Lord sends your ways His God Ordained men and women who will see the beauty in what seems insignificant in your life in The Name of Jesus Christ. May the fresh oil of God The Almighty touched the Christians everywhere to make each and every one of us to start appreciating the gift of God we carry in The Name of Jesus Christ.

A good example of willingness to start with your God's given idea was when the disciples wanted to feed five thousand souls, the disciples response to Jesus was "we have nothing here but five loaves and two fish" (Matthew 14:17) and Jesus did not say oh what a shame, what are we going to do with five loaves compare to the numbers of crowd, but rather Jesus said "bring them to me"

I encourage the reader of this book to take that good idea into the Lord in prayer, to start developing good attitude towards God and towards man, and to be willing to start using the Godly resources deposited into your care. To start improving on your gifts and talents, and may the Lord God release into your life divine strength to start doing something significant to the glory of His Name in The Name of Jesus Christ. Destiny killers shall no longer come your way in The Name of Jesus Christ. The Lord will placed in your life people like Elisha who will see the best of God in you, who will guide you into the blessings of the Lord. God will not send your way those who will kill your dreams in The Name of Jesus Christ.

The brothers of David tries to kill his dream, they are pleased with him taking care of the sheep somewhere in the field, but God empowered David to rise above their opinions of him, God empowered him to take his stands. May God empowers someone to be more daring in the face of every wrong voices of condemnations in the Name of Jesus Christ. Satanic attacks shall not have powers over you in The Name of Jesus Christ. May the whole Nations rise up to see the glory and the beauty of God in you. May the Lord empowers you to release what you have for His increase in The Name of Jesus Christ. Evil counsellors shall not come your way in The Name of Jesus Christ. Just the way Joseph did not take offence at his brothers that tried to kill his dream, so God will empowers someone not to take offence at anybody that has tried to cross their ways in The Name of Jesus Christ. May The Lord empowers you not to take offence at anyone, but rather to pray for their well beings in the Name of Jesus Christ. May The Lord empowers you with Wisdom to work with those that thought you are nothing in The Name of Jesus Christ. For those God is calling into the ministry, may the Lord empowers them to accept responsibilities in The Name of Jesus Christ. Souls shall no longer waste in our land, FRESH OIL of God the Almighty will rest on souls everywhere in The Name of Jesus, evil counsels shall be far from each and every one of us in The Name of Jesus Christ.

You may not be able to do everything, but there is something you can do that will release the blessings of the Lord into your life. Do not wait until when you can do everything, my idea of writing books started with studying the Word of God for several years, then it led into writing notes manually for years, before it leads to writing them using the Word Processors. You do not need to wait until when you can do everything, start with what you can do and stop listening to the voices that tells you how you can't, and just in case they tries to throw you out of one enterprise, God will lead you into a better one. The fear satan has used to paralyse its captives for several years is the fact that they cannot do certain things, the fear of making them to feel incompetent, satan will make sure that if possible he will not allow them to see what they can do but only what they cannot do, or he may tell them they are now too old, they shouldn't worry about life, satan is a liar and a father of liar, satan is a deceiver and its powers has been broken and defeated several years ago by our Lord and Saviour Jesus Christ .

.......He was a murderer from the beginning and does not stand in the truth, because there is no truth in him. When he speaks a falsehood, he speaks what is natural to him, for he is a liar [himself] and the father of lies and of all that is false (John 8:44)

Satan may tell its captors, they should wait until they gets into the promised land, or it may tell them they should not bother since they have no one to help them or that they are too old, we must thank God for the victory of boldness we have in Christ. We thank

God who saved us from the tongues of men. We thank God for the blood of Jesus that wiped away every ordinances that were against us. We thank God who daily loads us with His Wisdom, God did not leave anyone without talents except those that satan may deceive to make them feel that what they have is not enough. The lies of satan was broken two thousand years ago when Jesus went on the cross, paid the price on our behalf and declares us victorious.

What You Have is Not Too Small

Even if your assignment is to feed the nation, trust God to provide for you, God that supplies the assignment is capable of supplying the seed.

A seed as small as that of a mustard seed is what is required to become somebody in life. Remember when the disciples went to Jesus and asked Him to increase their faith, Jesus response was that, they should go and start using the faith they've got, that is the only way for any gift and talent to increase, you have to start using the resources God has given you, you have to expect that it will increase and produce some good results.

To study how Jesus described The Kingdom of God and how we can improve and increase the gifts of God within us ... (Study Luke 13:19)

SAY THIS OUT LOUD: I can do all things through Christ who strengthens me (Philippians 4:13)

NO REGRETS IN THE NAME OF JESUS CHRIST

*Put out into the deep [water], and lower
your nets for a haul (Luke 5: 4b)*

Have you tried an idea and it seems as if it doesn't work, try it again, the Bible advises that we should ask and keep asking until our joy is full, and even when your joy is full, keep asking until your joy starts overflowing to others. No one is self-sufficient, but just in case you are, get more wealth and become a distributor of God's wealth.

The story of the fishermen in the book of (Luke 5 1-10) is a good example that we must be determined never to give up. The fishermen in the story had gone down from their boats and were washing their nets, they have toiled day and night and caught nothing. In the midst of their resting from their hard labours that

54

generated no good results, God showed up in their case and encouraged them to try again, but this time to apply a better approach, and thank God, the fishermen tried and obey God's commands, the Bible wrote that they caught great number of fish to the extent their nets start breaking and the blessings overflows to those around them. Therefore, may I encourage you not to give up on that dream yet, listen to what God will say to you and obey.

You will not walk away without any blessings after a good dedicated tasks in The Name of Jesus Christ, your works shall have good rewards in The Name of Jesus Christ.

God knows who you are, He will singled you out for blessings in The Name of Jesus Christ. He will protect that which concerns you in The Name of Jesus Christ. Your labour will not be a waste.

SAY: Nations shall see the blessings and the faithfulness of God in me. The Lord God will bless me with riches that announces itself, the blessings that cannot be denied is my inheritance in The Name of Jesus Christ.

Chapter 5

BECOME AN ENCOURAGER

*Behold, how good and how pleasant it is
for brethren to dwell together in
unity.............for there the Lord has
commanded the blessing, even life
forevermore [upon the high and the lowly]
(Psalm 133: 1&3b)*

Where the Spirit of The Living God dwells, the Bible says there is liberty, where the Spirit of the Living God dwells, everyone is blessed, where the Spirits of The Living God dwells there is no difference between the Jews and the Greeks, it is the same God over all.

While we all desired to be encouraged as we pursue our God's given visions, may I encourage someone to also desire to become an encourager to others as they pursue their God's given assignments too, the Bible encourages us to give, and it shall be given unto us, the enemy of our soul knows that there is power in it if brothers can dwell together in unity. Hence he will try to set up souls to start competing with one another unnecessarily, but we thank God for the blood of Jesus that sets us free from every unhealthy competitions. We thank God for His Word that ministers to us daily, we thank God for the healing we received daily in the Body of Christ. We thank God for healing our land, we thank God for the salvations of souls. We thank God for the ability to hear Him through His Word, we are grateful that God has no shortage of blessings, heavens bank account is full, we thank God for destroying the works of satan for our sakes. We thank God for the Victories we have in Christ Jesus. We thank God for the abilities to follow His Word. We thank God for being saved, because God will revealed to us what satan is trying to do and He will show us a way of escape to safety in The Name of Jesus Christ.

Psalm 133 encourages us to dwell together in unity, for where there is love and harmony, God will put his blessings. God will not entrust the destiny of generations in the hands of someone or those who will squander it through strife, hence, we should avoid strife whenever it raises its ugly heads around us.

Celebrate God all day, every day. I mean, revel in him! Make it as clear as you can to all you meet that you're on their side, working with them and not against them (Philippians 4:4) **The Message**

Behold, how good and how pleasant it is for brethren to dwell together in unity! It is like the precious ointment poured on the head, that ran down on the beard, even the beard of Aaron [the first high priest], that came down upon the collar and skirts of his garments [consecrating the whole body]. It is like the dew of [lofty] Mount Hermon and the dew that comes on the hills of Zion; for there the Lord has commanded the blessing, even life forevermore [upon the high and the lowly] (Psalm 133: 1-3)

Dwelling together in unity according to Bible is like an ointments, it is like oil, it is like a balm that heals wounds, it is like the anointing oil for progress, it is like an anointing oil for Godly Wisdom, it is like the oil that lubricates, it is like the oil that makes a journey become smoother and better, it is for empowerment, dwelling together in unity empowers making a good progress in our God's given assignments.

Dwelling on the Word of God can help terminate the spirit of strife from entering into our lives, it can makes the weapons of satan not to work in our lives, and it can empower us to deal wisely in all things. It will bring us to maturity. It will increase our productivity levels in all good deeds.

So, since satan knew that it will be more profitable for us if we dwell in unity, it may tries to make sure that souls lives in strife. We thank God for The Word of God that advices us that we are not ignorant of satans devices, because God has revealed satans intentions to us through His Words, we choose to live at peace with all men, we refused to dwell on the ignorance satan is throwing at us to cause strives among us. And we applied the oil of God into our lands for every souls to be healed from every forms of wounds in The Name of Jesus Christ and we declare that the blessings that belongs to us will look for us at every corners in the Name of Jesus Christ.

Souls will have plenty of prosperities everywhere, no one will need to quarrel due to lack of any good things in The Name of Jesus Christ, and the peace of God will reign in our lives and in our lands in The Name of Jesus Christ. The love and the joy of the Lord will abounds in our lives in The Name of Jesus Christ. Souls everywhere shall have surplus prosperities and we shall almost wonders what to do with them, because the blessings will be so much in abundance.

I pray that our attitudes and speeches will not hinder anyone from becoming the best God has ordained them to be in The Name of Jesus Christ. I pray that the Lord will empowers us to learn to wait on Him in The Name of Jesus Christ. We received the Fresh Oil, we received the Godly Wisdom, and we received the empowerment to become a Good Encourager to God's people in the Name of Jesus Christ. Nations will say because of us they made heavens that is what will be our reports in The Name of Jesus Christ. We shall not become the tools in the hands of satan to stop the blessings of The Lord in the lives of His people, we shall not become an easy target for satan to use. We received the Wisdom to follow those You have assigned for us to follow in The Name of Jesus Christ. We choose to follow the Word of God on a daily basis without getting tired, without wavering in The Name of Jesus Christ.

PRAYER

From today I uproot every seed of discords that satan have sowed unnecessarily in our lands in The Name of Jesus Christ. Nations shall celebrates us, Nations shall celebrates the readers of this book in The Name of Jesus Christ. Every wrong veils of satanic prides is been removed from our lives in The Name of Jesus Christ. Whatever will not make us to start enjoying the best life God purposed for us is been removed in The Name of Jesus Christ. The Lord God will empowers us to be people's person as He ordained us to be in The Name of Jesus Christ. Satan shall no longer striped apart families and friends in The Name of Jesus Christ, satan shall no longer rule in our lands in The Name of Jesus Christ.

SHUT THE DOORS TO DOUBTS

Allow only the Word of God to keep flowing to you if you truly wants to attain to the blessings God purposed for you, keep away from anything or anyone that keeps reminding you that you are not capable of having the best God planned for you, keep away from them, shut the doors.

Chapter 6

FOLLOW GOD WHOLEHEARTEDLY

You will guard him and keep him in perfect and constant peace whose mind [both its inclination and its character] is stayed on You, because he commits himself to You, leans on You, and hopes confidently in You. So trust in the Lord (commit yourself to Him, lean on Him, hope confidently in Him) forever; for the Lord God is an everlasting Rock [the Rock of Ages] (Isaiah 26:3-4)

Breaking the Generation Curses

The Story in Numbers 32: 6-42 is a story where God broke generation curses from the lives of some tribes of Israel, their leader Moses reminded them about the attitudes of their parents of not having faith to follow God wholeheartedly, and the same kind of spirit was about to overtake the children i.e. the sons of Gad and of Reuben (see Numbers 32:6) He

63

reminded them by asking them the reason why they will be sitting down idle while their brethren go to war? While they should be passive when they should be active.

I pray that no one among us will be an easy target for satan in the Name of Jesus, the spirit of doing nothing will no longer be our portion in the Name of Jesus Christ. The Lord God will silence for each and every one of us every satanic embargoes in The Name of Jesus Christ. The Lord God will lead us into our own lands in The Name of Jesus Christ. The wrong voices of "you are not good enough shall be permanently silenced in the Name of Jesus Christ" The Spirit of lack of consistency in things that pertains to life and Godliness is broken in The Name of Jesus Christ.

Some of us, our parents worked hard all their lives from generations to generations, therefore, working hard is not enough if Christ is not at the centre of what we are doing. Following God wholeheartedly is to accept Christ as our Lord and Saviour and allowing His Words to dwell in us richly, to make up our mind that our commitment to the cause of Christ will get better day by day, and that there is no other God except Jesus Christ. The war that God requires for some of us to go may be to study the Word of God and allows it to dwell in us richly and to become a doer of the Word of God.

Thank God for the response from sons of Gad and of Reuben, there response was "we will not return to our homes until the Israelites have inherited every man his inheritance" (Numbers 33:18) the sons of Gad and of Reuben has acquired their own inheritance at that particular time in their journey, but God put a good spirit in them to go to the war to help their brothers and sisters (the Israelites) to come to their own inheritances. May Good leader's increases in our midst, who will not fight for their own inheritances alone, but to see that everyone is truly blessed in The Name of Jesus Christ. Also, the sons of Gad and Reuben mentioned that though they will go to war so as to bring the Israelites into The Promised Land, but they will not contend with them to take the blessings away from them, because they know where their own inheritances falls (see Numbers 32:19-42, 34: 13-15)

SERVING DOES NOT MEAN TAKING OVER

We must be willing to go and offer helping hands wherever God is sending us without taking over the ownership of what God has not given to us. We must remember that it is not at all the times God wants us to contend over inheritances. It is lack of trust and faith in God that He can bless that can make anyone to think that they must start quarrelling on what they are not likely going to get, especially if it is between two Christians. We must always trust God for our own blessings, knowing that whatever blessings that comes from God shall be a permanent blessings, this kind of attitude shows that we have conquered greed, and it is a way to avoid strife's in our land and a good way to preserve our own inheritances and the blessings. I love the Wisdom God gave unto the sons of Gad and of Reuben in Numbers 33 to agree to go to the war to break the generation curses of lack of perseverance, lack of focus and lack of the spirit of continuity which has plagued their family for generations, (see Genesis 49:1-4) and at the same time agreed to be content with their own inheritances, by so doing no one lacks or loses his inheritances among all the twelve tribes of Israel(Numbers 34:13-14) This is not to discourage us from receiving a qualified gifts approved by God, but it will save us from chasing winds and fighting battles that has no rewards. If sons of Gad and of Reuben refused to arm themselves for battles as God commanded, they would have perished just like their previous descendants but thank God for giving them an obedient spirit to obey God. What we are trying to drawn from this story is that we should seek the face of God for Wisdom to know when to be an encouragers to others or not, to know if our attitude is promoting the spirit of unity, love and blessings God desired or not, the truth we know is what will set us free:

And Moses said to the sons of Gad and of Reuben, Shall your brethren go to war while you sit here? Why do you discourage the hearts of the Israelites from going over into the land which the Lord has given them? Thus your fathers did when I sent them from Kadesh-barnea to see the land! For when they went up to the Valley of Eshcol and saw the land, they discouraged the hearts of the Israelites from going into the land the Lord had given them. And the Lord's anger was kindled on that day and He swore, saying. Surely none of the men who came up out of Egypt, from twenty years old and upward, shall see the land which I swore to Abraham, to Isaac, and to Jacob, because they have not wholly followed Me. Except Caleb son of Jephunneh the Kenizzite and Joshua son of Nun, for they have wholly followed the Lord. (Numbers 32:6-12)

The Bible advices that no one can have anything except it is first and foremost given unto him from above, also, that except the Lord build the house, he who labour labours in vain. I pray that God Almighty will empowers us to honour our leaders, the Lord God will empowers us to study His Word to discover the truth that will make us free. The Lord God will empowers us to follow His Words wholeheartedly in The Name of Jesus Christ.

Prayer

Lord God, empower us with your wisdom to serve effectively, knowing that it is You we are actually serving and that our rewards will come from you. Thank You Lord God for empowering us to make You to be our sources and our Provider for all things.

WILLINGNESS TO FIGHT THE GOOD FIGHT OF FAITH

The Bible advices that whatever your hands finds to do in goodness, do it. No task is too little and no tasks is too great. We must all be prepared to accept our God's given responsibilities, we must not settle for a life of passivity's, we must evaluate our lives regularly to see if we are making progress in our God's given assignment or not, we must not despise the days of the small beginnings. The sons of Gad and Reuben accepted to armed themselves before the Lord, ready to enter the land of Cannan for battle so as to preserve their inheritance and their action resulted into them being blessed (Numbers 32:31-42) which confirms the Bible verses that we should seek first the Kingdom of God and His righteousness first and every other things shall be added unto us (Matthew 6:33). Being armed for war may mean to study the Word of God and submit to what it says.

Jesus said, Truly I tell you, there is no one who has given up and left house or brothers or sisters or mother or father or children or lands for My sake and for the Gospel's. Who will not receive a hundred times as much now in this time—houses and brothers and sisters and mothers and children and lands, with persecutions—and in the age to come, eternal life (Mark 10: 29-30)

Also, see Matthew 19:29 and Luke 18:29

WE THANK YOU LORD GOD FOR BESTOWED ON US THE SPIRIT OF GOING FORWARD, THE SPIRIT OF UNITY, THE SPIRIT OF LEADERSHIP AND THE WILLINGNESS TO HELP OTHERS NOT BECAUSE OF WHAT WE WILL GET FROM THEM BUT SIMPLY DOING YOUR WILL. We thank You for The Wisdom of doing good so that someone may benefit from it especially in the household of faith. Whatever chains has tied anyone down unnecessarily trying to stop them from pursuing their God's given assignments is broken in The Name of Jesus Christ. The veils of satanic prides, idleness is broken from our lives and family and from the lives of the readers of this book in The Name of Jesus Christ.

If the sons of Gad and of Reuben refused to follow God, their actions would have had adverse effect on the whole tribes of Israel:

For if you turn from following Him, He will again abandon them in the wilderness, and you will destroy all this people (Numbers 32:15)

It is good to understand what God is saying at every seasons of our lives, the time to keep a good covenant with God and allowed His Words to guide us into all truth is not the time to be lazy, passive, taking things easy so as not to rock the boats, God is the only one to fear and His Words should always be our guide in all things especially if the blessings will be for the benefit of each and every one of us eventually.

SAY THIS OUT LOUD: Generation curses is broken from my life. I received the Wisdom to accept Godly responsibilities in The Name of Jesus Christ.

PUT ON THE WHOLE HARMOUR OF GOD and it will empowers you to run and not faint in all your activities to serve God.

Chapter 7

GO FORWARD

You have roamed around this mountain country long enough... (Deuteronomy 2:3)

Choosing not to go forward in our God's given assignment can have an adverse consequence on our lives and in the lives of those around us. Whenever God gives an assignments, it is not usually so as to bless just a single person, most of the God's given ideas is usually to bless you and everyone that surrounds you, and therefore it is good to obey God. Remember the story of the servant in the Bible who was about to be made redundant by his master, are you not thrilled by what he did, he quickly went to all his masters creditors and told them to pay what they can, instead of him losing his job and all the creditors, he applied some wisdom to the whole situation, he was willing to work harder, eventually, his master was delighted in him, hence the bible says "wisdom is the principal things.

No one that puts his hands in the plough and keeps looking back is fit for the Kingdom of God, I pray that the Lord God will give us The Wisdom to focus and to persevere in His assignment for us in The Name of Jesus Christ.

YOU SHALL NO LONGER BEG FOR GODS BLESSINGS BUT GOD WILL MAKE YOU TO BECOME THE GIVER.

THE MIRACLES AND THE BLESSINGS THAT WILL MAKE NATIONS TO WONDER SHALL locate you in the Name of Jesus Christ.

THE MIRACLES THAT CHANGES SOMEONE FROM THE BEGGER TO THE GIVER, MAY IT LOCATE SOMEONE TODAY.

THERE IS NOW NO CONDEMNATIONS TO THOSE WHO ARE IN CHRIST JESUS.

The story in John 9 began with a man tagged blind, his blindness was from his birth, and the Disciples of Jesus asked Jesus, who sinned that the man was born blind and without the knowledge of Christ, was it his parents or him, who is to be blame for his lack of the knowledge of God, who is to be blamed for the man's blindness.

Most of us have asked the question several time we see people that lacks the Wisdom of God, and Jesus response to them was that no one sin, we cannot blame anyone for the challenges people faced at times or for the fact that they did not discover the Word of God on time. The challenge the man in the story saw was to bring out in him the manifestation of the power of God, it is to show everyone that God still heals, that God can save anyone. "The man was born blind that the workings of God may be manifested through him". I am sure many of us has been through some challenges that almost made everyone around us to wonder why, but as they are wondering and some almost sympathises with us, so will they witness our miracles in The Name of Jesus Christ.

SOMEONE MAY ASKED ME, WHAT IS THE BEAUTY BEHIND THE STORY IN JOHN 9?

The beauty behind the story is the fact that Jesus knew that the man was blind and he needed healing from Him, instead of curing him straightaway, Jesus emphasised something special by saying "We must work the works of Him Who sent Me and be busy with

His business while it is daylight; night is coming on, when no man can work" (John 9:4) and I loved the word "We", which means that God wants all His children to be busy doing something meaningful for Him and towards our own blessings, and The Jesus Word was what led us to more scriptures in the Bible about being DILIGENT DOING SOMETHING GOOD:

Whatever your hand finds to do, do it with all your might, for there is no work or device or knowledge or wisdom in sheol (the place of the dead), where you are going. I returned and saw under the sun that the race is not to the swift nor the battle to the strong, neither is bread to the wise nor riches to men of intelligence and understanding nor favour to men of skill; but time and chance happen to them all (Ecclesiastes 9: 10-11)

Love one another with brotherly affection [as members of one family], giving precedence and showing honour to one another. Never lag in zeal and in earnest endeavour; be aglow and burning with the Spirit, serving the Lord. Rejoice and exult in hope; be steadfast and patient in suffering and tribulation; be constant in prayer. Contribute to the needs of God's people [sharing in the necessities of the saints]; pursue the practice of hospitality. Bless those who persecute you [who are cruel in their attitude toward you]; bless and do not curse them (Romans 12: 10-14)

If Jesus can be busy with the works of Him Who sent Him, what is He saying to us? Never be lazy, never be lag in zeal whilst serving the Lord.

Therefore, I do not know what your ailments is, but whatever it is, be encouraged, your perfection is in Christ and your perfection is here now.

Before Jesus cured the man, he advised all His listeners not to be lazy, He advised them to work whilst it is day time, the night is coming, when no man works, the Bible advices us that whatever good business and enterprises your hands finds to do, do it, be diligent in your profession.

Jesus eventually cured him and it astonished all his neighbours, because people knew him as a beggar, his miracles caused a bit of controversy between his neighbours, because, they can hardly recognised him now, so will it be for everyone trusting God for diverse miracles in The Name of Jesus Christ. The kind of miracles that change destiny from being a beggar to the Giver will locate you and me in The Name of Jesus Christ.

THE KIND OF BLESSINGS THAT ANNOUNCES ITSELF, THE BLESSINGS THAT MAKES NATIONS TO STAND IN AWE OF GOD, THE NOTABLE MIRACLES IS MY PORTION IN THE NAME OF JESUS CHRIST.

THE NAME OF JESUS SHALL BE EXALTED IN MY LIFE AND IN MY SITUATIONS IN THE NAME OF JESUS CHRIST. THE WORD OF GOD HAS WORKED WONDERS FOR ME AND IT IS STILL WORKING WONDERS DAILY IN MY SITUATIONS.

ALWAYS SHOUT THE NAME OF JESUS

Always acknowledged the Name of Jesus and allowed the system to expel you from their systems, allowed some organisations to expel you from their synagogue.

As you go about manifesting Christ, Nations may want to tag you as anything, do not be offended, a servant is not greater than his master, if they do it to Jesus, they may want to try it on you too by calling you all kinds of name.

The spirit of fear that tries to crippled souls from testifying of Christ is broken in The Name of Jesus Christ.

> *So we, numerous as we are, are one body in Christ (the Messiah) and individually we are parts one of another [mutually dependent on one another]. Having gifts (faculties, talents, qualities) that differ according to the grace given us, let us use them [He whose gift is] prophecy, [let him prophesy] according to the proportion of his faith. [He whose gift is] practical service, let him give himself to serving; he who teaches, to his teaching. He who exhorts (encourages), to his exhortation; he who contributes, let him do it in simplicity and liberality; he who gives aid and superintends, with zeal and singleness of mind; he who does acts of mercy, with genuine cheerfulness and joyful eagerness. [Let your] love be sincere (a real thing); hate what is evil [loathe all ungodliness, turn in horror from wickedness], but hold fast to that which is good. Love one another with brotherly affection [as members of one family], giving precedence and showing honour to one another. Never lag in zeal and in earnest endeavour; be*

aglow and burning with the Spirit, serving the Lord. Rejoice and exult in hope; be steadfast and patient in suffering and tribulation; be constant in prayer. Contribute to the needs of God's people [sharing in the necessities of the saints]; pursue the practice of hospitality. Bless those who persecute you [who are cruel in their attitude toward you]; bless and do not curse them. Rejoice with those who rejoice [sharing others' joy], and weep with those who weep [sharing others' grief]. Live in harmony with one another; do not be haughty (snobbish, high-minded, exclusive), but readily adjust yourself to [people, things] and give yourselves to humble tasks. Never overestimate yourself or be wise in your own conceits. Repay no one evil for evil, but take thought for what is honest and proper and noble [aiming to be above reproach] in the sight of everyone. If possible, as far as it depends on you, live at peace with everyone. Beloved, never avenge yourselves, but leave the way open for [God's] wrath; for it is written, Vengeance is Mine, I will repay (requite), says the Lord. But if your enemy is hungry, feed him; if he is thirsty, give him drink..................................... Do not let yourself be overcome by evil, but

*overcome (master) evil with good (Romans
12: 5-21)*

*Pray at all times (on every occasion, in
every season) in the Spirit, with all
[manner of] prayer and entreaty. To that
end keep alert and watch with strong
purpose and perseverance, interceding in
behalf of all the saints (God's consecrated
people) (Ephesians 6:18)*

FORGIVING OTHERS IS A GOOD WAY TO GO FORWARD.

The Bible advices us to be readily forgiving people
their offences towards us before they offend us at all,
which means that we must make forgiving people
their offences towards us our daily practice, we must
know that it is possible for human being to make
mistakes or to offend us, offence should not be a
thing of surprise to us again, we must be expecting
our one hundred perfection from God only. We must
not allow satan to use offence to stop our blessings
any longer. The Father God gave us the good
examples in the book of Genesis when Adam and
Eve did what they are not supposed to do, God

covered them immediately and He cursed satan for their sakes, He promised to send them a deliverer.

Also in the book of Genesis 6:3 God mentioned that He will not forever strife with man for he is flesh:

> *Then the Lord said, My Spirit shall not*
> *forever dwell and strive with man, for he*
> *also is flesh (Genesis 6:3)*

God wants us to learn from Him and received our healing from every binding spirit in the Name of Jesus Christ. Therefore, before anyone offend us, we must settle it in our mind that we shall not store the pains of offence in our body, and the Bible advices us that no weapons formed by satan will have authority over us in The Name of Jesus Christ.

Chapter 8

FORGET YOUR PAST MISTAKES

........but one thing I do [it is my one
aspiration]: forgetting what lies behind
and straining forward to what lies ahead
(Philippians 3:13b)

In order to go forward and truly achieved the greater height God purposed for you, do not give satan the permission to keep playing in your mind how you made mistake yesterday or sometimes ago, do not allow satan to keep reminding you about what you did not do right in the days of your training, forget about the past mistakes, forget about anyone you offended and the ones who offended you. Learn from your mistakes and moved on.

If you do not want to make a mistake in life, then do nothing, no one is perfect on this planet, everyone is learning daily how to do things better, how to please our master Jesus Christ. The Bible says that our master can be touched with the feeling of our infirmities, do not allow satan to keep flogging you about what went wrong somewhere in your Christian walks, if anything was wrong, it can be corrected. If there is nothing like mistakes, no one will send their children to school to go and learn, because everyone would have known everything.

Apostle Paul encourages us by saying to his brethren that not that he has reached his final attempt in doing greater things for God, but one thing he will do, forgetting about the past and pressing on for the better lifestyle in Christ Jesus. I think we all ought to be able to say that our best days are not behind us but in our future to attain.

If anyone has robbed you of your blessings in any way, allow God to avenge you, do not give room for any pain to linger in your memory forever, received your healing by letting go and let God in The Name of Jesus Christ.

The Bible advices us that we should not be afraid of any giant whatsoever, not to be afraid of anything that has made itself to look like giant before us especially the giants of unemployment's, the feelings of the lack of finances, the feeling of not having enough qualifications, whatever our needs may be, God is able to supply them abundantly in The Name of Jesus Christ. There is a saying that Rome wasn't built in a day, those that seems to have gone ahead of us did not get there one day, they only took the advantages of the opportunities presented to them and they kept developing it until it starts looking great to all of us.

FOCUS

If you too can focus on your God's given assignments you will get there, and you will be surprised to see what God can do with your talent that seems insignificant to you, and your life shall become a wonder to those that thinks nothing good will come out of your situations. The transformation God brought into the life of the man in John 9 was so significant, it threw the whole city into a state of confusion, God can do the same for anyone, allow the Word of God to renew your mind and if satan is trying to remind you about how you made a mistake sometimes ago, reminds satan that, that was then, we don't live in the past, we live in the now. The past mistakes were just the ways of discovering and learning how not to do certain things in life.

Whilst, we are in this world, mistakes may happens, but we must not allow mistakes to become our God.

We must settle it in our mind that God can perfect that which concerns us in The Name of Jesus Christ, therefore be free in your spirit, do not allow anything to hold you in the bondage of the mistake of the past consciousness. Be delivered from the spirit of perfectionism.

SCRIPTURES ON FORGIVENESS

Blessed (happy, fortunate, to be envied) is he who has forgiveness of his transgression continually exercised upon him, whose sin is covered. (Psalm 32:1)

For this [forgiveness] let everyone who is godly pray—pray to You in a time when You may be found; surely when the great waters [of trial] overflow, they shall not reach [the spirit in] him (Psalm 32:6)

So let it be clearly known and understood by you, brethren, that through this Man forgiveness and removal of sins is now proclaimed to you. (Acts 13:38)

SAY TO YOURSELF: I shall not dwell on my past mistakes anymore.

The Bible advices us that if anything is of good reports, think about them and fixed your minds on the Word and the blessings of the Lord, not on errors that satan threw on your ways.

For the rest, brethren, whatever is true, whatever is worthy of reverence and is honourable and seemly, whatever is just, whatever is pure, whatever is lovely and lovable, whatever is kind and winsome and gracious, if there is any virtue and excellence, if there is anything worthy of praise, think on and weigh and take account of these things [fix your minds on them]. Practice what you have learned and received and heard and seen in me, and model your way of living on it, and the God of peace (of untroubled, undisturbed well-being) will be with you (Philippians 4: 8-9)

If the Bible says FORGET IT, it may become a sin to dishonour the Word of God, if the Bible says forget it, then it will be a good thing to forget the past errors and keep pressing towards the best God has for you. It will be a good thing to let go of the past errors speedily, quickly as possible by not making it your dwelling places.

That was the reason why Jesus in the story of the woman caught in adultery asked her accusers, whoever is not guilty of the same offence among them should be the first to throw the stone at her, no one among them could throw the stone because they might have been more guiltier of the same offence more than her, no human being will tell you that they are guilty of the same offence in which they are trying to accuse you, you are the one who will not allow anyone or anything to run you down unnecessarily.

Honour the Word of God, received it personally, allow the Word of God to heal you of all the past wounds, meditate on it until you see its good manifestations in your life.

DO NOT ALLOW DISTRACTIONS

Keep away from anything that tries to unsettle your spirit, once you discovered that you don't feel alright after tuning in to some programs, then watch out not to tune in to them next time, avoid every ungodly chatting's and programs, pay more attentions to your own business and do not be overly too busy in another man's field except you are an employer of the company, do not allow any wrong programs or thinking to dominate you, to the extent of allowing it to start having an adverse effects on your health. God promised to keep in perfect health whose minds stays on Him.

Do not be anxious about anything, anxiety can throw your emotions up and down unnecessarily, cast all of your cares on God. No one can satisfy people as such on this planet, bear that in mind, just make your own contributions and allow others to make theirs.

Also see the book of Isaiah about forgetting the past mistakes

Do not [earnestly] remember the former things; neither consider the things of old. Behold, I am doing a new thing! Now it springs forth; do you not perceive and know it and will you not give heed to it? I will even make a way in the wilderness and rivers in the desert (Isaiah 43:18-19)

CHAPTER 9

BE EXPECTANT

For the Lord your God is bringing you into
a good land….. (Deuteronomy 8:7a)

After you have endured all sorts of hardships, after you have kept the God's commandments, be expecting good rewards to come to you. (See Deuteronomy 8:7-10) Obeying and serving God carries with it a good reward, be very conscious of the truth that God's blessings and prosperities will come to you in this life and in the one to come in The Name of Jesus Christ.

It may not come as quickly or rapidly as you want, if it is slow in coming, wait for it, be expecting it, it will surely come, and it will not be delayed (see Habakkuk 2)

What Should You Be Expecting You May Asked?

A Good Land

A Land of Brooks of Water

A Land of Fountains and Springs, flowing forth in valleys and hills

A Land of wheat and barley

A Land of vines and fig trees and pomegranates

A Land of olive trees and honey

A Land in which you shall eat food without shortage

A Land in which you shall not lack anything good

A Land whose stones are iron and out of whose hills you can dig copper.

See Deuteronomy 8:7-9

I pray that we shall be able to say "Lord, we are ready for Your assignment for us"

> *I have strength for all things in Christ Who empowers me [I am ready for anything and*

*equal to anything through Him
Who infuses inner strength into me; I
am self-sufficient in Christ's sufficiency]
(Philippians 4:13)*

BOOKS AUTHORED BY FOLAKE HASSAN

God is Good

We All Have Reasons to Praise God

The Names of God

The Attributes of God

Coming Out of Bondage

Be Encouraged

BECOMING A CHRISTIAN

Becoming a Christian is not a difficult task at all. The Holy Bible instructs every mankind to be born again by confessing our sin and accept Jesus Christ as our Lord and Saviour by praying a simple prayer of salvation.

The Prayer of Salvation

Father God, I come to You in the Name of Jesus Christ. According to your Word in the book of Roman 10:9, which says ''If you acknowledge and confess with your lips that Jesus is Lord and in your heart believe (adhere to, trusts in, and rely on the truth) that God raised Him from the dead, you will be saved.

I confess Jesus Christ as my Lord and Saviour, Lord Jesus come into my life and forgive me for all my sins. Be Lord of my life in Jesus name, Amen.

Congratulations if you have just prayed this prayer, you are now a Christian and you are saved.

You now have rights to all the promises of God in the Holy Bible.

I will advise you to read the Holy Bible and other Christian literatures regularly to build up your faith in the Lord. Also you will need a Word based church to attend regularly.

Be part of a good local church that teaches Christian to grow in The Word of God.

*****Please write to us to inform us of your new decision you made to become a Christian and we will continue to offer all helps necessary for you to grow in Christ.

Remain Blessed

Yours in Christ

Folake Hassan (Mrs)

Founder/President: The Blessed Christian Centre

ABOUT THE AUTHOR

Folake Hassan is the Author of the books titled "The Attributes of God", "Coming Out of Bondage" and several other books. She is the Owner of The Online Christian Bookshop named The Blessed Christian: www.theblessedchristian.co.uk . It is Folake's passion to see souls saved and confess Jesus Christ as their Lord and Saviour. Folake Hassan is blessed with 3 children with the youngest being 18 years of age at the time of writing this book. Folake and her children live in London, United Kingdom